IN THE NAME OF GOD
THE COMPASSIONATE, THE MERCIFUL

TREASURY OF WISDOM

Hossein Ansari Pour

Book Title: Treasury of Wisdom
Commissioned by the Office for the Management of Foreign Pilgrims of the AQR,
Islamic Relations Office
Published by the Islamic Propagation Department of the AQR
Translation and Commentary by Hossein Ansari Pour; 1979 CE
First Edition: 2018 CE/1439 AH
Graphic Artist: Zahra Subeiti, Mohamad Javad Taheri
Circulation: 3000
Printed by Quds Cultural Institute
ISBN: 978-622-6090-26-1

عنوان کتاب: حکمت های نهج البلاغه
به سفارش: مدیریت زائرین غیر ایرانی آستان قدس رضوی
ترجمه و شرح: حسین انصاری پور
چاپ اول: ۱۳۹۷ هش
طراح: زهرا سوبیتی، محمد جواد طاهری
چاپ : موسسه فرهنگی قدس
ناشر: معاونت تبلیغات اسلامی آستان قدس رضوی
شمارگان: ۳۰۰۰
شابک: ۱-۲۶-۶۰۹۰-۶۲۲-۹۷۸

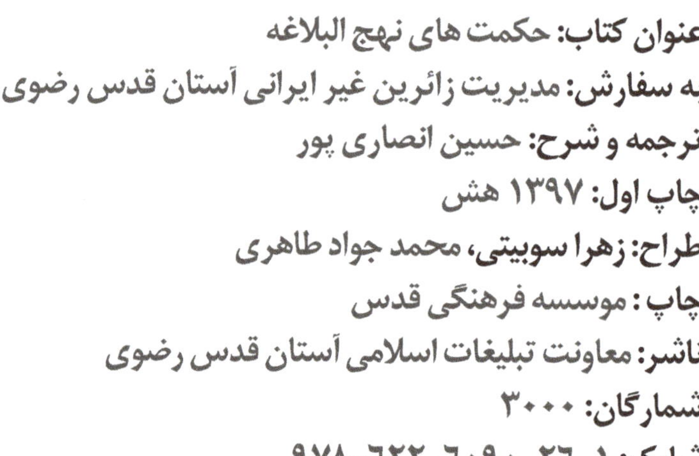

سرشناسه: علی بن ابی طالب (ع)، امام اول، 23 قبل از هجرت- 40 ق
Ali bin Abi Talib (P.B.U.H.), Imam I, 600-661

عنوان قراردادی: نهج البلاغه، انگلیسی، برگزیده

عنوان و نام پدیدآور:

Treasury of Wisdom/ Commissioned by the Office for the Management of Foreign
Pilgrims of the AQR/ Translation and Commentary by Hossein Ansari Pour

مشخصات نشر: 1397-2018 The Islamic Propagation Department of the AQR.

مشخصات ظاهری: 44 ص، مصور (رنگی) 29 × 22 س م.

شابک: 978-622-6090-26-1 رایگان

وضعیت فهرست نویسی: فیپا

یادداشت: انگلیسی

موضوع: علی بن ابی طالب (ع)، امام اول، 23 قبل از هجرت- 40 ق.—کلمات قصار
موضوع: Ali bin Abi Talib (PBUH), Imam I, 600-661—Quotations

موضوع: علی بن ابی طالب (ع)، امام اول، 23 قبل از هجرت- 40 ق.—نهج البلاغه-اخلاق
موضوع: Ali bin Abi Talib (PBUH), Imam I, Nahj ul-Balagha, Ethics

موضوع: اخلاق اسلامی—کلمات قصار
موضوع: Islamic Ethics—Quotations, Maxims, etc

شناسنامه افزوده: آستان قدس رضوی، مدیریت زائرین غیر ایرانی
شناسنامه افزوده: Astan Qods Razavi | The Management of Foreign Pilgrims

شناسنامه افزوده: انصاری پور، حسین، مؤلف
شناسنامه افزوده: Ansari Pour, Hossein

رده بندی کنگره: BP38/49522 1397

رده بندی دیویی: 297/9515

شماره کتابشناسی ملی: 5356604

Contents

Publisher's word

In the name of God, the Lord of Mercy, the Compassionate

'Abdullāh bin Ṣāliḥ al-Harawī narrates that Imam al-Riḍā (peace be upon him) had said, "'May God have mercy on the one who revives our tenets." I then asked him, "How can one revive your tenets?" "Through learning our knowledge and teaching it to others; If people find out about the merits of our words, they will certainly follow us", the Imam replied.'[1]

'Uyūn Akhbār al-Riḍā (pbuh), vol 1, p 307

One of the great forms of God's grace and kindness towards us is His bestowal of the Infallible Imams (pbut) upon us so that we may learn how to lead a Godly life through observing their way of life and eventually achieve eternal prosperity through practising their valuable instructions.

The city of Mashhad is a piece of heaven as it is home to the son of the Messenger of God (pbuh) who is the eighth star in the sky of Imamate. Every year millions of passionate pilgrims from around the world and other parts of Iran come to this spiritual sanctuary in order to quench the thirst of their souls by drinking from the limpid spring of the guidelines of the Infallible Imams (pbut).

Each one of those serving at the Holy Shrine of Imam al-Riḍā (pbuh) is in one way or the other serving the respected pilgrims of Imam al-Riḍā (pbuh) so that such they may make their pilgrimage with peace of mind whilst being able to benefit from this heavenly shrine.

In line with the above, the Office for the Management of Foreign Pilgrims at the Holy Shrine of Imam al-Riḍā (pbuh) has also been making every effort to introduce in various ways the way of life of Ahl al-Bayt (pbut)–and that of Imam al-Riḍā (pbuh) in particular–to the followers and devotees of this doctrine.

The measures taken by this office are in line with propagating the Islamic civilisation and culture appropriate to the needs and requirements of foreign pilgrims in order to provide them with insight and spiritual growth. Such measures take place in conjunction with the remarks made by the Supreme Leader of the Islamic Republic of Iran and the instructions given by the custodian of the Holy Shrine of Imam al-Riḍā (pbuh) while at the same time taking into account the provisions stipulated in the Twenty-year Outlook Document of the Holy Shrine of Imam al-Riḍā.

Some of the examples of the efforts made by this office in line with serving the foreign pilgrims of Imam al-Riḍā (pbuh) in the international sphere are as follows:

1- Holding special cultural programmes
2- Holding regular seminars on Islamic knowledge known as 'Circles of Knowledge'
3- Holding academic conferences

---

1. «عَنْ عَبْدِ السَّلَامِ الْهَرَوِيّ، عَنِ الرِّضَا (عليه السلام)، قَالَ: «رَحِمَاللَّهُ عَبْداً أَحْيَا أَمْرَنَا»، قُلْتُ: كَيْفَ يُحْيِي أَمْرَكُمْ؟ قَالَ: «يَتَعَلَّمُ عُلُومَنَا وَ يُعَلِّمُهَا النَّاسَ، فَإِنَّ النَّاسَ لَوْ عَلِمُوا مَحَاسِنَ كَلَامِنَا لَاتَّبَعُونَا.»

4– Holding educational classes and workshops
5– Holding cultural competitions and contests
6– Holding poetry readings
7– Holding conversion ceremonies for new converts to Islam
8– Responding to letters received from pilgrims
9– Dispatching books and other cultural products to all over the world
10– Responding to religious enquiries
11– Offering live internet interaction at Razavi Talk
12– Publishing the best of Islamic literature in several languages in the form of authored and translated books

It has been for some time that the call of Islam is echoing in every corner of the world with the hope of bringing people back to the truth to which they have been a stranger while at the same time inclinations towards Islam and the tendency of hearts towards seeking the truth is growing rapidly throughout the world.

We hope that the seekers of truth would find this book a useful and informative read and that it would be a step in the right direction as far as increasing the knowledge of pilgrims and devotees of the Infallible Imams (pbut) are concerned. Finally, we hope that this work would bring about the pleasure and satisfaction of the Glorious God.

O God, bless Muḥammad and Muḥammad's Household, provide me with a sound guidance which I seek not to replace, a path of truth from which I swerve not, and an intention of right conduct in which I have no doubts! Let me live so long as my life is spent in obeying you.

The Office for the Management of Foreign Pilgrims
The Holy Shrine of Imam al-Riḍa (pbuh)

Author's word

The book before you is comprised of a selection of forty words of wisdom from the renowned and profound book Nahj al–Balāgha, or otherwise known by its English equivalent as the 'Peak of Eloquence.' The Nahj al–Balāgha is a compilation of sermons, letters and maxims attributed to the renowned seventh–century Islamic figure, 'Alī bin Abī Tālib (pbuh), widely known as the Commander of the Faithful. The book was originally compiled by the tenth–century Shia Muslim scholar and poet, Sayyid al–Sharīf al–Raḍī.

Imam 'Alī (pbuh) was the cousin and son–in–law of Prophet Muḥammad (pbuh) as well as being his rightful successor. Prophet Muḥammad (pbuh) has been famously narrated as saying, 'I am the city of knowledge and 'Alī is its gate.' In one of the maxims of Nahj al–Balāgha, Imam 'Alī (pbuh) says, 'Our souls become weary in the same way that [our] bodies become tired; thus seek unique words of wisdom for them [so that they may be refreshed].'

The book at hand, which is intended for Muslims and non–Muslims alike, seeks to provide its reader with such refreshment for the soul. For this reason, the forty maxims in this book have been selected in a way that every reader could relate to them and their corresponding commentaries, irrespective of their religious or cultural background. The succinct and insightful sayings used in this book mainly focus on moral and ethical values within a social and individual context, and thus are intended to provide the reader with some valuable moral precepts and pieces of advice that are indispensable for leading an honourable way of life.

Finally, I would like to thank the team at the Islamic Relations Office at the holy shrine of Imam al–Riḍā (pbuh) and in particular my dear brother, Sheikh Hojjat Modarresi, for their support and efforts in bringing out this work.

Hossein Ansari Pour
Mash'had
July 2017

SOCIALISE WITH PEOPLE

IN SUCH A WAY THAT THEY WOULD WEEP FOR YOU IF YOU DIE AND LONG FOR YOU IF YOU CONTINUE TO LIVE

1

If you treat others around you in a nice, caring and forgiving manner, you will soon turn into one of their close friends: someone they can trust and feel close to. Gradually, you will become one of their loved ones whereby they will yearn to see you and socialise with you so long as you are living amongst them. Likewise, they will be mournful and sorrowful should they learn one day that you have passed away. Weeping for someone's death and missing them during their lifetime are two honest and genuine signs of a loving relationship between individuals.

THE DOER OF GOOD IS BETTER THAN THE GOOD ITSELF, AND THE DOER OF EVIL IS WORSE THAN THE EVIL ITSELF

Good and evil on their own are merely abstract notions that would only become real and concrete through the actions of individuals who carry them out. We all know what is good and what is bad, but knowing them is one thing and doing them is another. The person who performs a good deed is, in fact, transforming a good notion from an abstract form into a practical one, without whom the good notion would have otherwise remained lifeless. Hence such a person is obviously better than the good itself as they have given life to a lifeless concept.

The very same applies to the doer of evil.

THE WORTHIEST
OF ALL PEOPLE IN
FORGIVING
IS THE MOST CAPABLE OF THEM IN
PUNISHING

There are many forgiving people out there who forgive others for their mistakes and misdeeds. However, most of such people forgive because that is the next best thing they can do. They do not have any other options available to them. Real forgiveness manifests itself when one forgives others despite having the means and power to retaliate or punish them. In other words, the most forgiving of all people is the one who has the option of vengeance at their disposal, yet opts for forgiveness.

THE ONE
WHO WARNS
YOU ABOUT
SOMETHING
IS SIMILAR
TO THE ONE
WHO GIVES
YOU GOOD
NEWS.

When someone warns you about something, it indicates that they genuinely care about you and do not wish to see you hurt or harmed in any way. In other words, they are technically preventing something terrible from happening to you. So instead of possibly feeling upset or offended by such words of warning, one should be delighted and thankful to the warning individual in the same way that they would feel happy and grateful towards the bearer of good news.

FORGOING
A NEED IS
EASIER
THAN
SEEKING IT
FROM THE
WRONG
PERSON.

Sometimes we are in need of something that we cannot afford or provide on our own, and thus we may ask someone else for it. In such circumstances, it is essential to take into consideration towards whom we are going to extend a needy hand. If asking for something that we need is going to be followed by humiliation, degradation and dishonour because the helping person is belittling and demeaning us or laying an obligation on us, then we may well be better off without any such help while trying to come to terms with our unfulfilled need.

DO NOT BE ASHAMED OF MAKING A SMALL DONATION AS DEPRIVATION IN ITSELF IS LESS THAN WHATEVER YOU CAN GIVE.
CHARITY

Sometimes we are very keen to make a donation or give to charity, but we do not do so because we presume that we do not have much to offer or that it would be embarrassing to make such a small donation. Such an assumption is certainly wrong! Give whatever you can whenever you can as every penny you give is going to make a difference in someone's life. Likewise, every penny you withhold is going to have an adverse impact on someone else's life, and that is nothing but deprivation and poverty.

YOU SHALL NOT SEE AN IGNORANT PERSON UNLESS AT ONE EXTREME OR THE OTHER

A wise and knowledgeable individual would usually pursue a path of moderation in their life. Such people would avoid exceeding the proper bounds. They would not overdo or overstate something, and likewise, they would not minimise or understate anything. One of the characteristics of those who show excessive and extreme behaviour is that they are usually led to the other side of the extreme through the course of time. In other words, they will be trapped in a cycle of extremism as extremes meet. All forms of extremism emanate from ignorance, unawareness and lack of knowledge.

TALKING BECOMES LESS
WHEN INTELLECT IS
PERFECTED

Those who are talkative usually make a lot of blunders because they tend to think less and talk more. Talking too much can lead to mistakes that are caused by not thinking carefully enough about what you are going to say, and this can make you look and sound foolish before others. However, if talking is coupled with thinking, there would be less of talking and in turn fewer or no mistakes. More thinking and deliberation will enhance your power of reason to the point that your talking would become less while at the same time being more to the point. That is precisely why we can see people of knowledge and distinction talking less than the rest of us.

HOW DIFFERENT THESE TWO TYPES OF ACTIONS ARE:
THE ACTION THE JOY OF WHICH DEPARTS
BUT ITS CONSEQUENCE REMAINS,
AND THE ACTION THE TROUBLE OF WHICH
DEPARTS BUT ITS REWARD REMAINS
17

Sometimes we engage in doing something that seems full of pleasure and enjoyment at the time of doing it, but then we would have to deal with the repercussions and consequences of that action for a lifetime. That is because we tend to only focus on the momentary pleasures without considering the long-term ramifications. In contrast, sometimes we go through a lot of difficulties and hardships to achieve something, but then we reap the rewards of our strenuous efforts for a lifetime. Wisdom dictates that we focus on the lingering consequences of our actions rather than the temporary and ephemeral pleasures.

THE ONE WHO APPROVES
OF THE ACTION OF A GROUP OF PEOPLE
IS AS THOUGH HE HAS TAKEN
PART IN THAT ACTION WITH THEM
19

Sometimes we do not physically take part in a particular action ourselves, but we feel a sense of satisfaction and gratification when we learn about a particular action that has been or is being committed by a group of people. In other words, we would be condoning their action or agreeing to it though we have not had any direct role in it. Those individuals who condone or applaud the evil deeds or atrocities committed by others are in fact accomplices in their crime and stand as guilty as them.

HE WHO EXPOSES HIMSELF TO SITUATIONS OF ACCUSATION SHOULD NEVER BLAME OTHERS FOR HAVING A POOR OPINION OF HIM.

Although we all know that being suspicious and judgemental about other people is not right, unfortunately, we see a lot of it in our communities and societies. Therefore, it is of paramount importance that we do not put ourselves in a position that would lead others to make assumptions about us or have a poor opinion of us. We cannot fully dismiss what people think about us and ignore their views if we are going to have a successful and meaningful presence in our society. It would be irresponsible of us to expect everyone to have a good opinion of us while being careless about how we conduct ourselves in society.

THE ONE WHO IS OPINIONATED SHALL PERISH, AND THE ONE WHO SEEKS ADVICE FROM MEN OF DISTINCTION HAS, IN FACT, BECOME A PARTNER IN THEIR INTELLECT

CON
SU
LTA
TION

The one who is obstinate and always proceeds independently in their decisions is bound to make huge mistakes sooner or later. In contrast, those who seek advice from others and consult them about their decisions and steps in life, tend to make fewer mistakes and achieve more success. When you rely solely on your own opinion and make decisions independently, you are relying on your own limited experience, but when you seek advice from others, you are sharing their experiences and knowledge with that of yours. Consultation helps you make a sound and sensible decision with no remorse or failure in sight.

PEOPLE ARE ENEMIES OF THAT WHICH THEY ARE IGNORANT ABOUT.

It is very easy to form an opinion about something of which we have no knowledge. Lack of knowledge and ignorance about other people or things could easily lead us to misunderstandings, misjudgements, misconceptions, etc. It could even lead to hatred and animosity. Therefore, one should not form an opinion about anything or anyone for that matter without actually knowing anything or having very little information about them. We should avoid being amongst those individuals who show enmity and hostility towards something or someone because they are simply unaware of the relevant facts.

WHEN YOU FEAR SOMETHING, THROW YOURSELF INTO IT AS THE SEVERITY OF BEING CONSTANTLY ON YOUR GUARD IS GREATER THAN WHAT YOU ARE **AFRAID OF.**

In certain stages of our life, we are faced with some risky challenges ahead of our way which could hold us back. Those who do not give in to fear and face such challenges head-on tend to move on to the next step in their life successfully, but on the contrary, those who are always fearful tend to lag behind and face failures. That is similar to a person who is afraid of going into the water because they do not know how to swim. However, they would not learn how to swim unless they first go into the water after which they would be able to learn a new skill by having overcome their fear.

REBUKE THE EVIL DOER
BY REWARDING
THE WELL-DOER

Those who do evil in a social context should certainly be brought to justice and reprimanded for their actions in order to prevent them from repeating the same misdeeds. However, sometimes we can reach this end differently by rewarding and celebrating those who do well and play a constructive role in society.

Imagine a teacher who has two students one of whom has properly completed their homework while the other one has failed to do so. Here the teacher has two options: either scold the student who has not done their homework or reward the student who has completed their homework. The latter would certainly encourage other students to follow the example of the praised student while at the same time dissuading others from failing to do their homework in future.

OBSTINACY
WITHDRAWS THINKING

An obstinate person is usually bent on their decision or choice to the extent that they would not allow any further contemplation and deliberation on the subject in question. Not only they will not give themselves the chance to review and assess their course of action, but their obstinacy and stubbornness would also prevent them from seeking advice from other individuals. Such persons usually have to deal with the repercussions of their thoughtlessness and recklessness throughout their entire life without ever being able to make up for the wrong decisions that have arisen from their obstinacy.

GREED

IS LIFELONG SLAVERY.

A person who has a constant and endless desire to have more and more would not stop at anything to achieve what they have in mind; even if that meant at the cost of their own dignity and honour. They would allow greed to overtake their dignity whereby they would accept any type of humiliation and disgrace before others in order to reach their desired goal. They will reach a point that it would be them serving their greed rather than their greed serving them. In other words, they will be enslaved for life by their own greed.

THE WEALTH
THAT HAS GONE,
BUT HAS TAUGHT
YOU A LESSON
HAS NOT REALLY
BEEN LOST.

Sometimes we may lose a certain amount of our money or property as a result of a decision we have made or an action we have taken. If we learn from our mistake and avoid repeating the same mistake that has led to such a financial loss, then we have not really lost anything. Money, wealth and property are deemed lost when we get nothing in return for spending them. However, if we learn a lesson from such expenditure, it would no longer be deemed a loss but a real gain and asset.

THE CAPACITY OF EVERY CONTAINER IS REDUCED BY WHAT IS PLACED IN IT EXCEPT THE CONTAINER OF

KNOWLEDGE

AS IT EXPANDS WITH MORE KNOWLEDGE.

A cup can only hold a certain amount of water in it, and once it is full, any extra water poured in it would flow over the edge of the cup. However, this does not apply to the container of knowledge. The more knowledge you add to your mind and intellect, the greater and larger your capacity for knowledge shall be as it keeps expanding to allow in more knowledge. Your mind as the container of knowledge shall never be filled. So one should never be under the assumption that they are immersed in knowledge as the more you learn, the more space will be available to be to filled with further learning and knowledge.

THE FIRST REWARD THAT A FORBEARING PERSON REAPS IN RETURN FOR HIS FORBEARANCE IS PEOPLE'S SUPPORT FOR HIM IN THE FACE OF THE IGNORANT

Our reaction can be very decisive when faced with an ignorant and uncouth person. If we react to them in the same way by insulting and offending them, we would be belittling ourselves by reducing our personality and character to the same level as theirs. However, if we deal with such insolent individuals through patience and forbearance, the first benefit that we will reap is that others around us will realise very quickly who is on the wrong side and will naturally take sides with us against the disrespectful person.

ONE'S SELF-CONCEIT
IS ONE OF THE ENVIERS OF
ONE'S INTELLECT

Someone who is envious of us because of our success and achievements in life could express their envy and jealousy towards us in many different ways. It could be in the form of a longing to have what we have achieved or a feeling of resentment towards our success. Such feelings of resentment and spitefulness on the part of the envious individual can affect us adversely.

Our intellect and wisdom are not an exception. Self-conceit or undue pride is one of the enviers of our intellect in the sense that it will show resentment and spitefulness towards us. In other words, self-conceit will not allow our intellect and power of reason to function in our best interest.

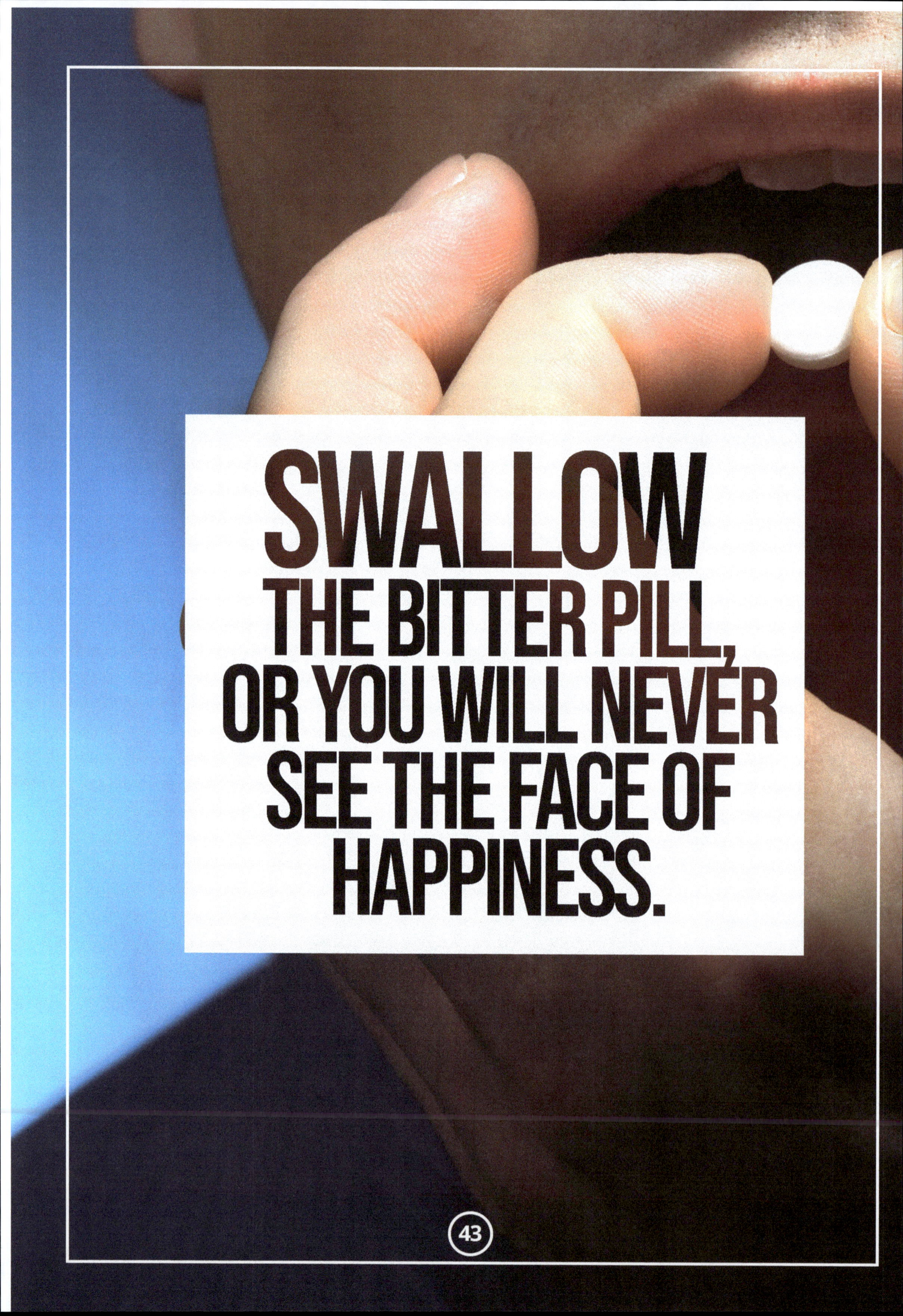

SWALLOW
THE BITTER PILL,
OR YOU WILL NEVER
SEE THE FACE OF
HAPPINESS.

None of us can ever claim that we have never gone through any hardships in our lives. We all have experienced some sort of hardship and difficulty in one way or the other. However, this should not hold us back from making an effort for a better tomorrow and having a brighter future. We must accept the severity and pain of what we have been through. We should deal with it and move on otherwise we would be depriving ourselves of the good days ahead of us. In other words, one should not cling to past misfortunes, or the future happiness will slip through their fingers.

THE ENVY OF A FRIEND
ARISES FROM AN AILING FRIENDSHIP
45

A true friend is one who would wish you what they would like for themselves and not wish you what they would dislike for themselves. In other words, a real friend would wish you the best at all times and feel genuinely happy for you in every success you achieve in your life. Likewise, they would feel genuinely sad for every failure you may face in your life. A real friend would never feel jealous or envious of your achievements and would always be there for you in times of difficulty. Anything but this would indicate a weak and poor bond of friendship.

MOST OF THE FAILURES OF INTELLECT ARISE FROM
THE GLEAMS OF GREED

When we are constantly focused on our material longings and desires, we tend to think less intelligently and wisely about the steps we take in our life. We would be so filled with greed and avarice that we would not realise the advantages and disadvantages of the choices and decisions we make in our life. Greed would overtake our power of reason and intellect, and this is one of the instances where one would believe that the end justifies the means. In other words, you would resort to any wrong or immoral practice in order to fulfil your greed and covetousness without ever considering the consequences.

GIVE CREDENCE
TO THE SUPPOSITION
OF THE ONE WHO THINKS WELL OF YOU

Sometimes we have to work very hard to give a positive impression of ourselves to others or win someone's trust, but sometimes we do not have to do that as we are fortunate enough to have someone who already thinks well of us and all we have to do is prove them right. In other words, if someone thinks well of you, then prove them right. Also, bear in mind that proving someone right is always easier than proving them wrong.

THE BEST OF JOBS IS THAT WHICH YOU COMPEL YOURSELF TO DO IT

Sometimes we may not necessarily enjoy undertaking a certain task, or it may prove tiresome and challenging, but then we proceed with it regardless when we take into consideration the forthcoming rewards. A job or work in which there is no diligence and perseverance will not usually bear many fruits. The harder you work and the greater your perseverance, the more fruitful and rewarding the results shall be. That is precisely why behind every successful work and every great achievement; there is always a strong resolve and will. As the 17th-century English poet, Robert Herrick, rightly attests, 'If little labour, little are our gains – Man's fate is according to his pains.'

RAGE IS A FORM OF INSANITY FOR IT IS FOLLOWED BY REMORSE ON THE PART OF THE VIOLENT. THUS, IF HE DOES NOT FEEL REMORSEFUL AFTERWARDS, IT WOULD ONLY MEAN THAT HIS INSANITY IS DEEPLY ENTRENCHED

When one is full of rage and fury, their power of reason and intellect is usually undermined by their rage and thus not allowing them to behave or act in a sensible and appropriate manner. Therefore, it could be argued that rage or violent anger affects one's sanity adversely as it prevents an individual from thinking reasonably and sensibly. This leads to a temporary period of insanity and irrationality that is usually followed by a sense of remorse after sanity takes over. However, there are some individuals who do not have this sense of remorse after showing violent anger, and this demonstrates that they are deprived of sanity and sagacity altogether.

A LITTLE OF SOMETHING IN WHICH YOU PERSEVERE IS MORE PROMISING THAN MUCH OF SOMETHING WHICH IS TIRESOME

Imagine someone who has just started going to the gym. If they start exercising long hours or overdo it, they could harm their health and feel disheartened about exercising altogether. However, if they start with shorter time slots and using lighter equipment, they would be able to keep it up and have a steady progress.

You should not impose doing something on yourself that is beyond your capacity or capability; otherwise, sooner or later you will give up on that task. Perseverance is undeniably essential to one's success but only at a reasonable and feasible pace. In other words, success is achieved through perseverance and steadiness combined.

BEING IN NO NEED OF MAKING AN EXCUSE IS MORE HONOURABLE THAN MAKING A VALID ONE

Sometimes we fail to fulfil a commitment, task or obligation as required after which we find ourselves in need of making an excuse or apology. It could also be something wrong that we have done or for having offended someone. Offering a legitimate excuse or a sincere apology would be something decent and appropriate for us to do, but it would have been much better if we had avoided putting ourselves in a situation that would lead us to making an apology. That is because even a valid excuse or a heartfelt apology would still make us lose a certain degree of our dignity and self-worth.

A PREACHER
WITHOUT
PRACTICE
IS LIKE AN
ARCHER
WITHOUT A
BOWSTRING.

A person who gives advice to other people on life issues and encourages them to behave in a particular way must make sure that they are already leading by example as far as their advice and exhortations are concerned. In other words, they must practice what they preach, or they would be portraying themselves as a hypocrite, and thus no one would take heed of their advice. People usually look to individuals who suit their actions to their words.

After all, actions speak louder than words.

THE GREATEST WEALTH
IS TO DESPAIR OF THAT WHICH IS
IN THE HANDS OF OTHER PEOPLE

Some people are constantly comparing what they have with those of others who seem to have more than them in terms of wealth and property. This would always give them a sense of lacking and dissatisfaction as they would always see themselves as being inferior to others. Always yearning for what others have can also lead to losing what you already have as you would never appreciate and value your own belongings and achievements. You would never feel prosperous and satisfied unless you start focusing on what you have regardless of what others may have. After all, being rich is not about having the most but needing the least.

YOUR SELF-RESPECT IS LIKE ICE THAT MELTS INTO DROPS BY BEGGING, SO BE MINDFUL AS TO BEFORE WHOM YOU LET IT MELT.
63

If you are in need of something and are going to ask for it from someone, make sure that you would be asking the right person otherwise your self-respect and dignity could be at stake. The right person is someone who would help you and give to you out of kindness and generosity, and without laying an obligation on you. Dealing with your needs and problems on your own would be a wiser option than having to ask the wrong person. Don't let your self-respect melt away easily.

THE ONE WHO LOOKS INTO HIS OWN FAULTS SHALL BE DISTRACTED FROM OTHER PEOPLE'S FAULTS.

Some individuals keep looking into other people's faults and mistakes and constantly criticise them either in person or behind their back. We all know that this is an inappropriate behaviour as no one is really perfect, but how can we avoid behaving in such an indecent manner? One of the most effective ways is for a person to look into their own faults and try to overcome and correct them rather than keeping an open eye for other people's shortcomings and inadequacies. Not being blind to your own faults shall make you blind to other people's faults and flaws.

THE ONE WHO
UNSHEATHES
THE SWORD OF
INJUSTICE SHALL
BE KILLED WITH IT

Those who wage unjust wars on other peoples and nations or those who treat other individuals aggressively and oppressively will someday have a taste of what their victims have gone through. In other words, what goes around comes around. Throughout human history, we can see despots, tyrants and oppressors – on both national and individual levels – who have had humiliating and defeating eventualities at the hands of their very own victims. The one who digs a pit will fall into it, and if someone rolls a stone, it will roll back on them.

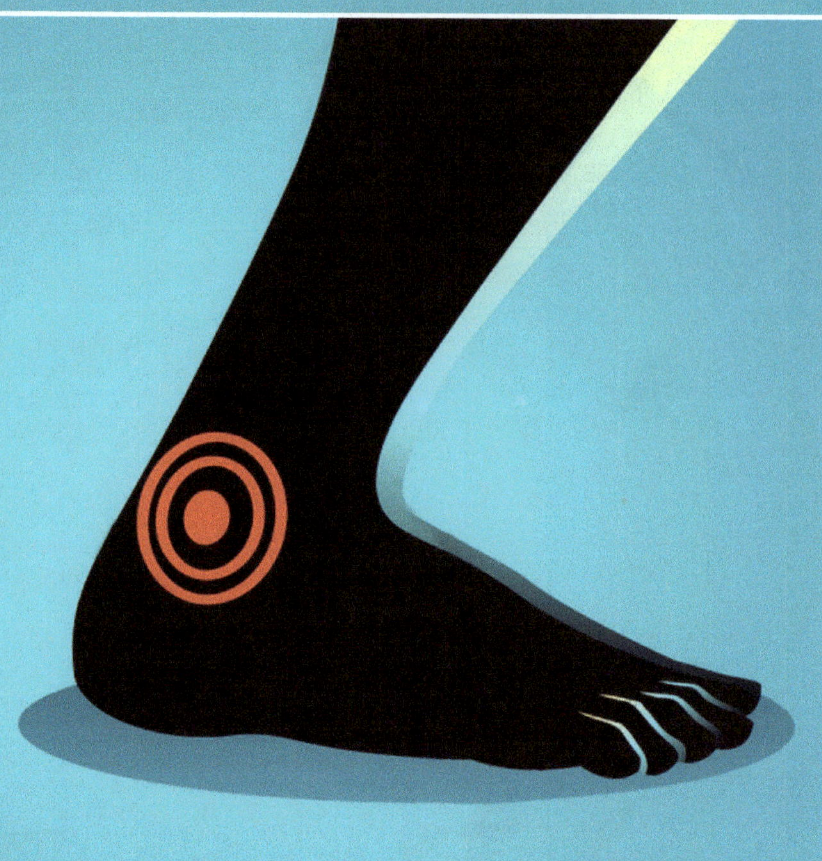

THE GREATEST FAULT

IS TO FIND FAULTS THE LIKES OF WHICH

CAN BE FOUND IN YOURSELF

Looking at other people's faults and inadequacies is already a reprehensible trait, but what is far worse is finding faults with other people the likes of which can already be seen in us. For instance, imagine an individual who is stingy and miserly but at the same time chides other stingy individuals for being tight-fisted. Such a person would be considering what is inappropriate for others to do as being good for themselves. Such paradoxical and hypocritical behaviour demonstrates a high degree of decadence in one's character.

WORDS
ARE IN YOUR SHACKLES
SO LONG AS YOU HAVE
NOT UTTERED THEM, BUT YOU
WILL BE SHACKLED BY THEM
ONCE YOU HAVE UTTERED THEM

It is of paramount importance that we think carefully before talking and watch every word that we utter. What is said is heard and what is heard can never be withdrawn. That is precisely why one of the deepest senses of remorse is felt after having said what you should not have said. One's tongue can be the most difficult animal to tame, and if not tamed and controlled, it could really prove detrimental to one's character and reputation. Some of our words can come back to haunt us for years to come should we get used to talking recklessly and negligently.

THE AVOIDANCE

OF THAT WHICH YOU DISLIKE IN OTHERS WOULD BE SUFFICIENT FOR

YOUR OWN EDIFICATION

Some people do not find it easy to see their own faults and shortcomings or they would not realise that they may have a bad trait or behaviour within themselves. However, they can easily notice the negative aspects of other people's behaviour. All such individuals would have to do is to see what they find unacceptable and inappropriate in other people's behaviour and try to avoid the very same qualities in themselves. In a way, this could be described as learning from other people's mistakes which can prove to be an efficient way of self-improvement and self-edification.

THERE ARE TWO TYPES OF PERSONS WHOSE INSATIABLE APPETITE IS NEVER SATISFIED: **THE SEEKER OF KNOWLEDGE** AND **THE SEEKER OF THIS WORLD**

People can be divided into two groups: those who solely seek worldly pleasures and usually cannot get enough of them and then those who seek knowledge and science who equally cannot get enough of learning. Both worldly desires and knowledge are limitless and without any end in sight. The more of worldly and material desires one gets, the more they would want and likewise the more knowledge one would gain, the more knowledge they would seek. However, the former can lead to greed and immoral practices while the latter would lead to wise and steady conduct in life.

BACKBITING IS AN ENDEAVOUR BY THE POWERLESS

Those people who suffer from jealousy, or those who bear a grudge against someone but find themselves unable to achieve what others have, or feel incapable of retaliation usually resort to backbiting. They talk behind other individuals' back due to a continuous failure to satisfy their own ego. They feel weak and powerless, and thus they behave like a person who does not have the strength and power to confront someone face to face and instead resorts to stabbing them from the back. However, a person who finds themselves as being capable and competent would rather explore other avenues without ever trying to tarnish other people's image and reputation in society.

FRUGALITY
IS THE WEALTH THAT
DOES NOT DWINDLE AWAY

A person who appreciates the value of their hard-earned money shall equally value frugality and simplicity in life. They would spend their money on what is necessary as opposed to spending extravagantly and lavishly on purchases that are beyond one's needs and requirements; purchases that have roots in endless greed and which will ultimately lead to wastefulness and profligacy. One of the greatest benefits of leading a frugal life is that one would always have enough money at their disposal to be able to fulfil their needs. On the other hand, those who spend carelessly and recklessly may someday realise that they do not have enough money even to fulfil their basic needs.

References

Page 1

خَالِطُوا النَّاسَ مُخَالَطَةً إِنْ مِتُّمْ مَعَهَا بَكَوْا عَلَيْكُمْ وَ إِنْ عِشْتُمْ حَنُّوا إِلَيْكُمْ

Socialise with people in such a way that they would weep for you if you die and long for you if you [continue to] live

Saying No 10 of Nahj al-Balāgha

Page 3

فَاعِلُ الْخَيْرِ خَيْرٌ مِنْهُ، وَفَاعِلُ الشَّرِّ شَرٌّ مِنْهُ

The doer of good is better than the good itself, and the doer of evil is worse than the evil itself

Saying No 32 of Nahj al-Balāgha

Page 5

أَوْلَى النَّاسِ بِالْعَفْوِ أَقْدَرُهُمْ عَلَى الْعُقُوبَة

The worthiest of all people in forgiving is the most capable of them in punishing

Saying No 52 of Nahj al-Balāgha

Page 7

مَنْ حَذَّرَكَ كَمَنْ بَشَّرَكَ

The one who warns you [about something] is similar to the one who gives you good news

Saying No 59 of Nahj al-Balāgha

Page 9

فَوْتُ الْحَاجَةِ أَهْوَنُ مِنْ طَلَبِهَا إِلَى غَيْرِ أَهْلِهَا

Forgoing a need is easier than seeking it from the wrong person

Saying No 66 of Nahj al-Balāgha

Page 11

لَا تَسْتَحِ مِنْ إِعْطَاءِ الْقَلِيلِ، فَإِنَّ الْحِرْمَانَ أَقَلُّ مِنْهُ

Do not be ashamed of making a small donation as deprivation in itself is less than that [which you can give]

Saying No 67 of Nahj al-Balāgha

Page 13

لَا تَرَى الْجَاهِلَ إِلَّا مُفْرِطاً أَوْ مُفَرِّطاً

You shall not see an ignorant person unless [he is] at one extreme or the other

Saying No 70 of Nahj al-Balāgha

Page 15

إِذَا تَمَّ الْعَقْلُ نَقَصَ الْكَلَامُ

Talking becomes less when intellect is perfected

Saying No 71 of Nahj al-Balāgha

Page 17

شَتَّانَ بَيْنَ عَمَلَيْنِ: عَمَلٍ تَذْهَبُ لَذَّتُهُ وَتَبْقَى تَبِعَتُهُ، وَعَمَلٍ تَذْهَبُ مَؤُونَتُهُ وَيَبْقَى أَجْرُهُ

How different these two types of actions are: the action the joy of which departs but its consequence remains, and the action the trouble of which departs but its reward remains

Saying No 121 of Nahj al-Balāgha

Page 19

الرَّاضِي بِفِعْلِ قَوْمٍ كَالدَّاخِلِ فِيهِ مَعَهُمْ

The one who approves of the action of a group of people is as though he has taken part in that [action] with themwhatch

Saying No 154 of Nahj al-Balāgha

Page 21

مَنْ وَضَعَ نَفْسَهُ مَوَاضِعَ التُّهَمَةِ فَلاَ يَلُومَنَّ مَنْ أَسَاءَ بِهِ الظَّنَّ

He who exposes himself to situations of accusation should never blame others for having a poor opinion of him

Saying No 159 of Nahj al-Balāgha

Page 23

وَمَنِ اسْتَبَدَّ بِرَأْيِهِ هَلَكَ، وَمَنْ شَاوَرَ الرِّجَالَ شَارَكَهَا فِي عُقُولِهَا

The one who is opinionated shall perish, and the one who seeks advice from men of distinction has, in fact, become a partner in their intellect

Saying No 161 of Nahj al-Balāgha

Page 25

النَّاسُ أَعْدَاءُ مَا جَهِلُوا

People are enemies of that which they are ignorant about

Saying No 172 of Nahj al-Balāgha

Page 27

إِذَا هِبْتَ أَمْرًا فَقَعْ فِيهِ، فَإِنَّ شِدَّةَ تَوَقِّيهِ أَعْظَمُ مِمَّا تَخَافُ مِنْهُ

When you fear something, throw yourself into it as the severity of being constantly on your guard is greater than what you are afraid of

Saying No 175 of Nahj al-Balāgha

Page 29

ازْجُرِ الْمُسِيءَ بِثَوَابِ الْمُحْسِنِ

Rebuke the evil doer by rewarding the well-doer

Saying No 177 of Nahj al-Balāgha

Page 31

اللَّجَاجَةُ تَسُلُّ الرَّأْيِ

Obstinacy withdraws thinking

Saying No 179 of Nahj al-Balāgha

Page 33

الطَّمَعُ رِقٌّ مُؤَبَّدٌ

Greed is lifelong slavery

Saying No 180 of Nahj al-Balāgha

Page 35

لَمْ يَذْهَبْ مِنْ مَالِكَ مَا وَعَظَكَ

The wealth that has [gone, but has] taught you a lesson has not [really] been lost

Saying No 196 of Nahj al-Balāgha

Page 37

كُلُّ وِعَاءٍ يَضِيقُ بِمَا جُعِلَ فِيهِ إِلاَّ وِعَاءَ الْعِلْمِ، فَإِنَّهُ يَتَّسِعُ

[The capacity of] every container is reduced by what is placed in it except the container of knowledge as it expands [with more knowledge]

Saying No 205 of Nahj al-Balāgha

Page 39

أَوَّلُ عِوَضِ الْحَلِيمِ مِنْ حِلْمِهِ أَنَّ النَّاسَ أَنْصَارُهُ عَلَى الْجَاهِلِ

The first reward that a forbearing person reaps in return for his forbearance is people's support for him in the face of the ignorant

Saying No 206 of Nahj al-Balāgha

Page 41

عُجْبُ الْمَرْءِ بِنَفْسِهِ أَحَدُ حُسَّادِ عَقْلِهِ

One's self-conceit is one of the enviers of one's intellect

Saying No 212 of Nahj al-Balāgha

Page 43

أَغْضِ عَلَى الْقَذَى وَ الْأَلَمِ تَرْضَ أَبَداً

Swallow the bitter pill or you will never see the face of happiness

Saying No 213 of Nahj al-Balāgha

Page 45

حَسَدُ الصَّدِيقِ مِنْ سُقْمِ الْمَوَدَّةِ

The envy of a friend [towards another friend] arises from an ailing friendship

Saying No 218 of Nahj al-Balāgha

Page 47

أَكْثَرُ مَصَارِعِ الْعُقُولِ تَحْتَ بُرُوقِ الْمَطَامِعِ

Most of the failures of intellect arise from the gleams of greed

Saying No 219 of Nahj al-Balāgha

Page 49

مَنْ ظَنَّ بِكَ خَيْراً فَصَدِّقْ ظَنَّهُ

Give credence to the supposition of the one who thinks well of you

Saying No 248 of Nahj al-Balāgha

Page 51

أَفْضَلُ الْأَعْمَالِ مَا أَكْرَهْتَ نَفْسَكَ عَلَيْهِ

The best of jobs is that which you compel yourself to do it

Saying No249 of Nahj al-Balāgha

Page 53

الْحِدَّةُ ضَرْبٌ مِنَ الْجُنُونِ، لِأَنَّ صَاحِبَهَا يَنْدَمُ، فَإِنْ لَمْ يَنْدَمْ فَجُنُونُهُ مُسْتَحْكِمٌ

Rage is a form of insanity for it is followed by remorse on the part of the violent Thus, if he does not feel remorseful afterwards, it would only mean that his insanity is deeply entrenched

Saying No 255 of Nahj al-Balāgha

Page 55

قَلِيلٌ تَدُومُ عَلَيْهِ أَرْجَى مِنْ كَثِيرٍ مَمْلُولٍ

A little of something in which you persevere is more promising than much of something which is tiresome

Saying No 278 of Nahj al-Balāgha

Page 57

الْاِسْتِغْنَاءُ عَنِ الْعُذْرِ أَعَزُّ مِنَ الصِّدْقِ بِهِ

Being in no need of making an excuse is more honourable than making a valid one

Saying No 329 of Nahj al-Balāgha

Page 59

الدَّاعِي بِلاَ عَمَلٍ كَالرَّامِي بِلاَ وَتَرٍ

A preacher without practice is like an archer without a bowstring

Saying No 337 of Nahj al-Balāgha

Page 61

الْغِنَى الْأَكْبَرُ الْيَأْسُ عَمَّا فِي أَيْدِى النَّاسِ

The greatest wealth is to despair of that which is in the hands of [other] people

Saying No 342 of Nahj al-Balāgha

Page 63

مَاءُ وَجْهِكَ جَامِدٌ يُقْطِرُهُ السُّؤَالُ، فَانْظُرْ عِنْدَ مَنْ تُقْطِرُهُ

Your self-respect is like ice that melts into drops by begging, so be mindful as to before whom you let it melt

Saying No 346 of Nahj al-Balāgha

Page 65

مَنْ نَظَرَ فِي عَيْبِ نَفْسِهِ اشْتَغَلَ عَنْ عَيْبِ غَيْرِه

The one who looks into his own faults shall be distracted from other people's faults

Saying No 349 of Nahj al-Balāgha

Page 67

مَنْ سَلَّ سَيْفَ الْبَغْيِ قُتِلَ بِهِ

The one who unsheathes the sword of injustice shall be killed with it

Saying No 349 of Nahj al-Balāgha

Page 69

أَكْبَرُ الْعَيْبِ أَنْ تَعِيبَ مَا فِيكَ مِثْلُهُ

The greatest fault is to find faults [with others] the likes of which can be found in yourself

Saying No 353 of Nahj al-Balāgha

84

Page 71

الْكَلاَمُ فِي وَثَاقِكَ مَا لَمْ تَتَكَلَّمْ بِهِ، فَإِذَا تَكَلَّمْتَ بِهِ صِرْتَ
فِي وَثَاقِهِ

Words are in your shackles so long as you have not uttered them, but you will be shackled by them once you have uttered them

Saying No 381 of Nahj al-Balāgha

Page 73

كَفَاكَ أَدَباً لِنَفْسِكَ اجْتِنَابُ مَا تَكْرَهُهُ مِنْ غَيْرِكَ

The avoidance of that which you dislike [to see] in others would be sufficient for your own edification

Saying No 412 of Nahj al-Balāgha

Page 75

مَنْهُومَانِ لاَ يَشْبَعَانِ: طَالِبُ عِلْمٍ، وَطَالِبُ دُنْيَا

There are two types of persons whose insatiable appetite is never satisfied: the seeker of knowledge and the seeker of this world

Saying No 457 of Nahj al-Balāgha

Page 77

الْغِيبَةُ جُهْدُ الْعَاجِزِ

Backbiting is an endeavour by the powerless

Saying No 461 of Nahj al-Balāgha

Page 79

الْقَنَاعَةُ مَالٌ لاَ يَنْفَدُ

Frugality is the wealth that does not dwindle away

Saying No 475 of Nahj al-Balāgha